Life Cycles

Pillbugs

by Donna Schaffer

Consultant:
Richard Mankin, Ph.D.
USDA—Agricultural Research Service
Center for Medical, Agricultural,
and Veterinary Entomology

Bridgestone Books
an imprint of Capstone Press
Mankato, Minnesota

Bridgestone Books are published by Capstone Press
818 North Willow Street, Mankato, Minnesota 56001
http://www.capstone-press.com

Library of Congress Cataloging-in-Publication Data
Schaffer, Donna.
    Pillbugs/by Donna Schaffer.
    p. cm.—(Life cycles)
    Includes bibliographical references (p. 23) and index.
    Summary: Describes the physical characteristics, habits, and stages of development
of one kind of isopod, the pill bug.
    ISBN 0-7368-0212-6
    1. Isopoda—Life cycles—Juvenile literature. [1. Wood lice (Crustaceans)] I. Title.
    II. Series: Schaffer, Donna. Life cycles.
QL444.M34S36 1999
595.3'72—dc21
                                                                    98-53029
                                                                         CIP
                                                                          AC

Editorial Credits
Christy Steele, editor; Steve Weil/Tandem Design, cover designer; Linda Clavel,
    illustrator; Kimberly Danger, photo researcher

Photo Credits
Bill Beatty, Cover
Dwight R. Kuhn, 10
Rob and Linda Mitchell, 8, 12, 16, 16 (inset), 20
Visuals Unlimited/Richard Walters, 4, 6, 18; Bill Beatty, 14-15

Table of Contents

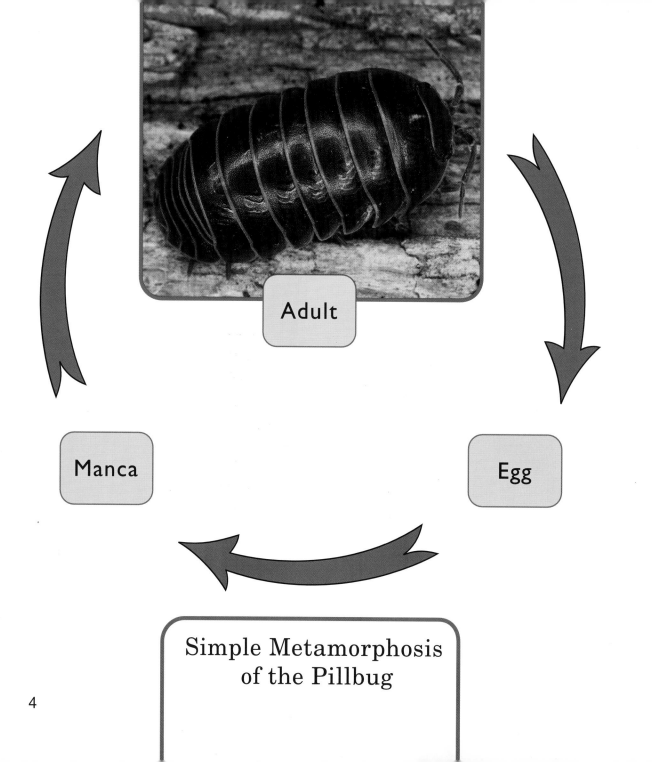

Adult

Manca

Egg

Simple Metamorphosis
of the Pillbug

The Life Cycle of the Pillbug

Pillbugs go through simple metamorphosis. Simple metamorphosis has three stages. A pillbug's body form changes three times.

Pillbugs grow in eggs during the first stage of simple metamorphosis. Pillbugs look much like adults when they hatch.

After pillbugs hatch, they are in the manca stage. Mancas do not have all their adult body parts. During this second stage, mancas develop adult body parts.

The third life stage of a pillbug's life is the adult stage. Adults are fully grown and have fully developed body parts.

These stages make up a pillbug's life cycle. Almost all living things go through cycles of birth, growth, reproduction, and death.

About Pillbugs

Pillbugs are small creatures that never grow more than 3/4 inch (1.9 centimeters) long. The tops of their oval-shaped bodies are curved and protected by hard plates. Their color ranges from brown to purple-gray. Pillbugs have flat undersides.

Pillbugs are not insects. Pillbugs are closely related to lobsters, crabs, and other water isopods. Pillbug is the general name for land isopods. All isopods have three body sections and seven pairs of jointed legs. Isopods have antennas and exoskeletons. These hard, outer coverings protect the isopods like a suit of armor.

Pillbug species have many nicknames. People call them potato bugs, wood lice, rolypolies, grammerzows, and cheeselogs.

About 4,000 isopod species exist. Each isopod species has its own features. But all isopod species have the same life cycle.

● ● ● ● **Pillbugs can roll their bodies into balls. The rolled-up creatures reminded people of pills. So people called the creatures pillbugs.**

Where Pillbugs Live

Pillbugs live in most areas of the world. They are found on all types of land. They live near ocean coasts, on mountains, and even in dry deserts.

Pillbugs make their homes in dark, moist places. They live under logs or stones. Pillbugs need moist conditions to survive. Their bodies can dry out quickly. Pillbugs in dry areas roll up to keep moisture inside their bodies. They also search for moist places to rest.

Pillbugs are cold-blooded. Their body temperature depends on the temperature around them. Pillbugs hide from the hot sun. Some pillbugs dig burrows in soil. These underground holes protect pillbugs from heat. Pillbugs come out at night when the air is cooler.

● ● ● ● **This species of pillbug lives in damp, dark caves. This pillbug has no eyes. Its two antennas help it move around, find food, and locate mates.**

Mating

Pillbugs go through several stages during their life cycle. Adult pillbugs are in the final stage of the life cycle. They mate and produce young.

Most pillbugs first mate when they are 1 to 2 years old. Pillbugs mate one to four times each year. Some pillbugs mate with only one other pillbug throughout their lives.

Pillbugs mate at night. A male climbs onto a female's back. He licks her head to make sure she tastes like a female pillbug. He also taps on her back with his legs. This tells the female pillbug that he is a male pillbug.

Some females lay a brood of eggs after mating. A brood may have up to 250 eggs. This large group of young begins the life cycle together.

● ● ● ● **Young pillbugs called mancas hatch from the eggs.**

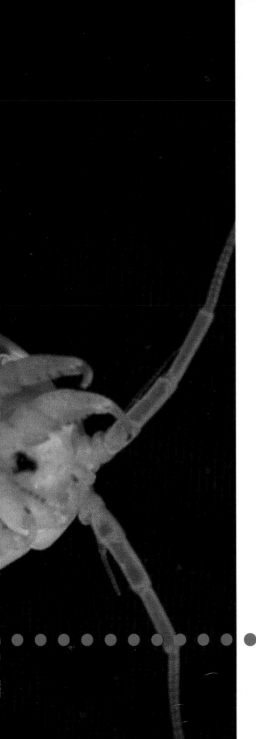

Brood Pouch

The egg is the first stage in a pillbug's life cycle. A pillbug grows inside the egg.

Females from some pillbug species have a special brood pouch to hold fully formed eggs. This liquid-filled sac is attached to the underside of the female's body. The brood pouch protects the eggs. Its liquid keeps the eggs moist.

Pillbugs grow inside the eggs for two to three months. The pillbugs hatch inside the brood pouch.

Females do not raise their young. Pillbugs are on their own as soon as they hatch and leave the brood pouch.

You can see this cave pillbug's brood pouch. The brood pouch is full of eggs.

Mancas

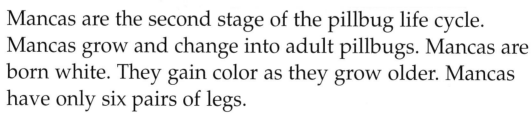

Mancas are the second stage of the pillbug life cycle. Mancas grow and change into adult pillbugs. Mancas are born white. They gain color as they grow older. Mancas have only six pairs of legs.

Mancas must molt to grow. They shed the exoskeletons that cover their bodies. Mancas first molt within 24 hours after hatching. Mancas grow their seventh pair of legs during this molt. They then are called pillbugs.

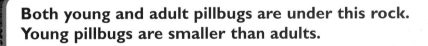

Both young and adult pillbugs are under this rock.
Young pillbugs are smaller than adults.

Molting

Pillbugs eat before they molt to store energy. This energy helps them grow into their new coverings. Pillbugs are ready to molt again when their coverings become tight and hard.

Isopods molt differently than most animals. Isopods shed only half their exoskeleton at one time. Other animals shed their whole exoskeleton at one time. Isopods shed the second half of their exoskeleton several days later.

Pillbugs stop eating one to two days before they molt. They usually find a place to hide from enemies. When pillbugs are molting, they cannot roll into a ball to protect themselves. Toads, frogs, birds, spiders, and other pillbugs eat pillbugs that are molting.

Pillbugs molt up to 12 times. Pillbugs grow and molt for one year before they become adults. Pillbugs may live for up to three years.

This pillbug has shed the back half of its exoskeleton. The inset photo shows that the pillbug's new covering is white and soft.

Pillbugs and Water

Some scientists believe that pillbugs once lived in water. Over time, pillbugs developed the ability to live on land. Some pillbugs have organs that breathe air. But others still breathe through gill slits like fish do. These body parts help pillbugs breathe by taking oxygen out of water.

Today, pillbugs still need water to survive. Pillbugs can die if they become too dry. The shape of a pillbug's body helps it collect water. Water drops roll down its curved upper body.

A pillbug can drink through its mouth. Pillbugs also suck up water through a body part called a uropod. The uropod is a tube that brings water to the gills. Pillbugs also take in water in other ways. They soak up water through the soft undersides of their bodies. This water moves to the gills. Pillbugs get water from their food too.

The pillbug's curved body helps it collect water.

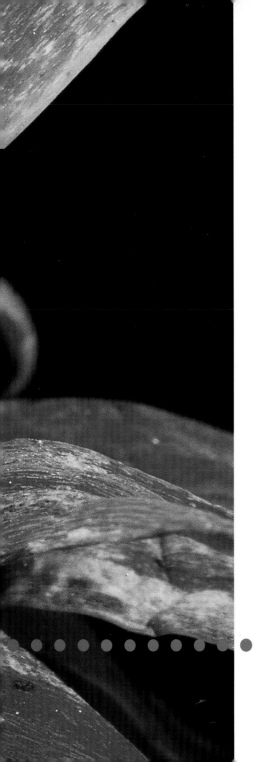

Pillbugs and Food

Most pillbugs eat rotting wood and plants. They sometimes eat living plants or dead animals. Pillbugs also will eat other pillbugs if there is not enough food. Pillbugs also may eat other pillbugs if too many live close together.

Pillbugs use their antennas to find food. They feel around and smell with their antennas.

After they find food, pillbugs eat it with their mandibles. They use these strong mouthparts to break food into small pieces.

Pillbugs help break down dead plants and leaves when they eat. This process helps new plants grow.

These pillbugs are eating a flower.

Hands On: Raise a Pillbug

Pillbugs are easy to raise. You can make a pillbug home and watch a pillbug throughout its life cycle.

What You Need

A large, clear plastic container   Dirt
Small leaves, twigs, and stones   Pillbugs
Lettuce or potato pieces   Water
A paper towel

What You Do

1. Place 1 inch (2.5 centimeters) of dirt in the container. Sprinkle some water on the dirt.
2. Put the leaves, twigs, and stones on the dirt.
3. Soak a crumpled paper towel in water. Place it in the corner of the container.
4. Place pieces of lettuce or potato in the container. Pillbugs will eat this food.
5. Put your pillbugs into their new home.
6. Put new food in once each week.
7. Rewet the paper towel every two weeks.

Words to Know

brood (BROOD)—a group of eggs

brood pouch (BROOD POUCH)—a liquid-filled sac on a female isopod's body where eggs are held and hatched

exoskeleton (eks-oh-SKEL-uh-tuhn)—a hard, bony covering on the outside of an isopod

gill slits (GIL SLITSS)—body parts in the sides of some isopods through which they breathe

isopod (EYE-suh-pod)—an animal that has seven pairs of legs, three main body parts, and an exoskeleton

manca (MAN-cuh)—a newborn pillbug; mancas are white and have only six pairs of legs.

mandibles (MAN-duh-buhlz)—strong mouthparts

molt (MOHLT)—to shed an outer covering so that a new one can grow

Read More

Morgan, Sally. *Butterflies, Bugs, and Worms.* Young Discoverers. New York: Kingfisher, 1996.

Ross, Michael Elsohn. *Rolypolyology.* Backyard Buddies. Minneapolis: Carolrhoda Books, 1996.

Useful Addresses

Department of Entomology
Royal Ontario Museum
Toronto, ON M5S 2C6
Canada

The Pillbug Project
National Science Teachers
   Association
1714 Connecticut Avenue NW
Washington, DC 20009

Internet Sites

The Bug Club
http://www.ex.ac.uk/bugclub

Wood Lice Facts
http://www.geocities.com/CapeCanaveral/Hangar/
   7649/wlice.htm

Index